THE RISE OF THE MUMMIES

by Hermione Redshaw

Minneapolis, Minnesota

Credits
Images are courtesy of Shutterstock.com. With thanks to Getty Images, Thinkstock Photo, and iStockphoto. 2–3 – shaineast, Marti Bug Catcher. 4–5 – Merydolla, Yevhenii Kornieiev, Prostock-studio. 6–7 – Jaroslav Moravcik, rocharibeiro, Pakhnyushchy. 8–9 – Andrea Izzotti, Jeremy Red. 10–11 – Kiselev Andrey Valerevich, Merydolla. 12–13 – Luis Louro, Fedor Selivanov, Robcartorres. 14–15 – Unique Vision, Sergei Kolesnikov, Mona Ahmed, Mark Carrel. 16–17 – Parilov, Christian Vinces. 18–19 – DerekTeo, Marco Porcu, bogdan ionescu. 20–21 – Geartooth Productions, Arlee.P, nasidastudio, Cosmin Manci. 22–23 – Motortion Films, Kiselev Andrey Valerevich. 24–25 – Krakenimages.com, PRPicturesProduction. 26–27 – Krakenimages.com, Angela Kotsell. 28–29 – eldeiv, ganjalex. 30 – givaga.

Bearport Publishing Company Product Development Team
President: Jen Jenson; Director of Product Development: Spencer Brinker; Managing Editor: Allison Juda; Associate Editor: Naomi Reich; Associate Editor: Tiana Tran; Senior Designer: Colin O'Dea; Associate Designer: Elena Klinkner; Associate Designer: Kayla Eggert; Product Development Specialist: Anita Stasson

Library of Congress Cataloging-in-Publication Data is available at www.loc.gov or upon request from the publisher.

ISBN: 979-8-88822-012-2 (hardcover)
ISBN: 979-8-88822-199-0 (paperback)
ISBN: 979-8-88822-327-7 (ebook)

© 2024 BookLife Publishing
This edition is published by arrangement with BookLife Publishing.

North American adaptations © 2024 Bearport Publishing Company. All rights reserved. No part of this publication may be reproduced in whole or in part, stored in any retrieval system, or transmitted in any form or by any means, electronic, mechanical, photocopying, recording, or otherwise, without written permission from the publisher.

For more information, write to Bearport Publishing, 5357 Penn Avenue South, Minneapolis, MN 55419.

CONTENTS

Arriving in Egypt 4

The Mummy's Curse 8

Tomb Raiding Kit 12

The Search for the Mummy 16

Inside the Tomb 18

Escape the Tomb 20

Life with the Mummy's Curse 24

Lifting the Curse 28

Surviving 30

Glossary 31

Index 32

Read More 32

Learn More Online 32

ARRIVING IN EGYPT

Welcome to Egypt. This is the land of **pharaohs**, pyramids, and . . . mummies!

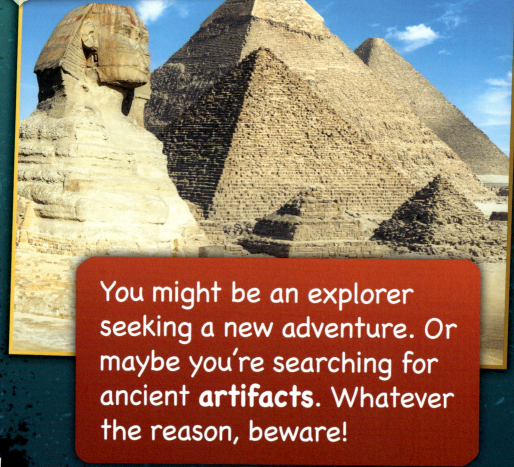

You might be an explorer seeking a new adventure. Or maybe you're searching for ancient **artifacts**. Whatever the reason, beware!

Exploring the past can be dangerous. Keep this guide close.

Before you go any further, let's learn about Egypt's history.

In **ancient** Egypt, the rulers were kings and queens called pharaohs. Pharaohs were treated well in life and in death!

Pharaohs were very powerful. Many people thought of them as gods.

When a pharaoh died, their body would be **mummified**. Their brain, lungs, liver, and stomach were removed. Then, their body was wrapped in cloth.

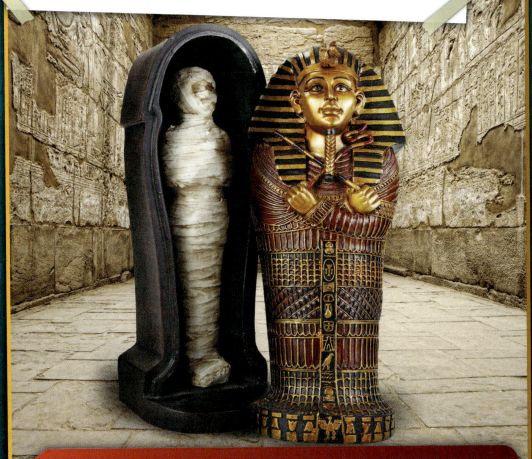

A pharaoh's mummy was buried in a **tomb** inside a pyramid. Treasure was also buried with the body.

7

THE MUMMY'S CURSE

You may really want to open a mummy's tomb to peek inside. Don't!

Ancient Egyptians believed if mummies were disturbed, the pharaohs would not reach the **afterlife**. Some tombs were filled with **booby traps** to keep the mummies safe.

And there are even some tombs that may have **curses**.

Curses are no joke! They have been said to cause everything from bad luck to illnesses . . . or worse!

Legends say that some curses bring mummies back from the dead. Then, the mummies seek **revenge** on the person who woke them.

Some curses are more feared than others. Are you ready?

The pharaoh Tutankhamun's tomb was found in 1922. King Tut, as he came to be known, had been buried for 3,000 years. When he was found, many of his treasures were removed.

Several strange deaths came soon after. Was this King Tut's curse or just bad luck?

TOMB RAIDING KIT

So, the curses haven't scared you off? If you still plan to explore tombs, be prepared.

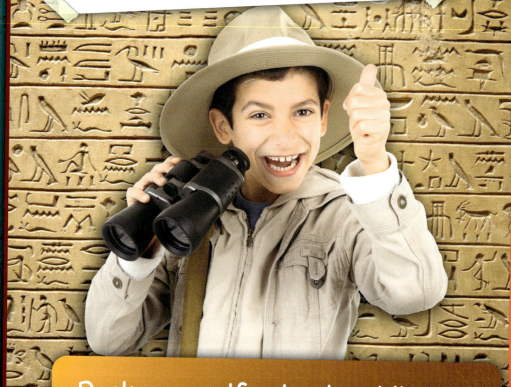

Pack yourself a tomb raiding kit. It may even help you escape the curse of a mummy's tomb!

LIGHT

It's dark deep inside a pyramid. Your kit will need a **torch** to help you see where you are going.

Watch out for traps!

You can also use a torch to protect yourself. Who knows what could happen inside a pyramid?

ROPE

What will you do if the floor crumbles under your feet? A rope could save you from falling into a deep pit!

Every kit should have a long, strong rope with a hook. You can use it to climb to safety.

The writing in ancient Egypt used hieroglyphs, or pictures that stood for words. They are often seen inside pyramids.

A hieroglyphic dictionary may help you read a message. Is it a helpful warning or a deadly threat?

THE SEARCH FOR THE MUMMY

Let's head to the biggest pyramid in Egypt. It's the Great Pyramid of Giza. This pyramid is more than 4,000 years old. Inside is the tomb of Pharaoh Khufu.

Stay alert!

Khufu's mummy and treasure have never been found. Maybe that's how he wants it!

The inside of pyramids can be built like mazes. Leave a trail behind you so you don't get lost.

Watch out! A brick that looks different from others might set off a booby trap.

INSIDE THE TOMB

There it is! You've found the tomb. The walls are covered in gold. There is a huge chest filled with Khufu's treasures in the middle of the room.

Be careful! The room could have traps. Move very slowly.

You found Khufu's coffin! If you feel brave, slowly push off the lid. Look at the mummy inside!

Khufu's mummy has an **amulet** on its chest. You pick it up for a closer look . . .

ESCAPE THE TOMB

Oh no! The room is cursed! It's time to go.

Quick! Grab the amulet and head for the exit.

The ground begins to shake. Try crawling along the floor so you don't fall.

Prepare for falling stones. Cover your head!

A scarab beetle

Stones might not be all that falls from the ceiling. Scary creatures might be up there, too. Watch out for snakes, scorpions, spiders, and scarab beetles!

As you run, you may feel the floor give way. If your legs begin to slide into the ground, it might be quicksand!

Your rope will help you here!

People can sink into quicksand very quickly. You will need to be fast.

You're almost out, but what's that horrible smell? Mummies are coming!

Don't let them touch you!

The mummies stumble around. They are still very weak. Run before they get stronger!

LIFE WITH THE MUMMY'S CURSE

Getting away from the pyramid may not be enough. What if the curse of the mummies follows you home?

Each curse is different. Let's look at some signs of a curse.

You might notice the food in your house gets moldy very quickly. This can make it very difficult to eat your dinner.

Until you have lifted the curse, stick to canned foods. They will last longer.

Sometimes, a curse causes lots of bad luck. This might mean failing a test, losing your homework, or tripping on steps.

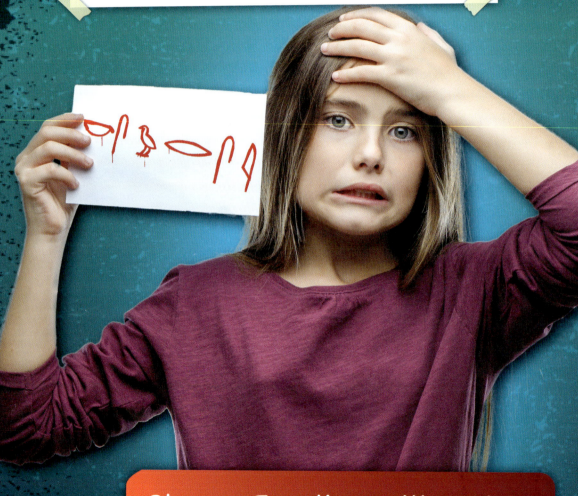

Strange Egyptian writing might also appear. You may see it on walls or in your notebook.

A curse can cause piles of sand to appear in odd places. Soon, you might see sand everywhere you go!

Try to avoid touching anyone else, even your annoying brother or sister. This will keep the curse from spreading.

LIFTING THE CURSE

You need help! Lifting a mummy's curse may seem difficult, but it is really very simple.

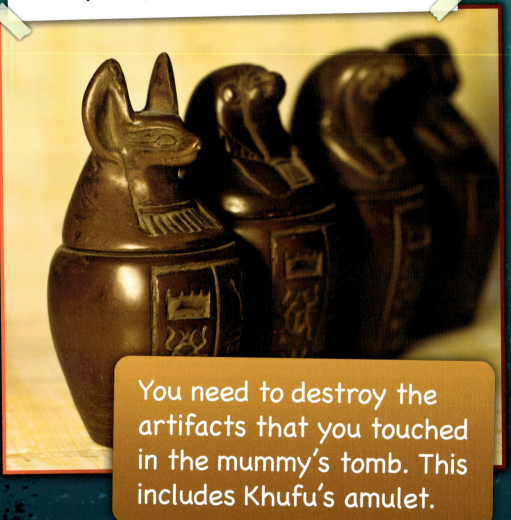

You need to destroy the artifacts that you touched in the mummy's tomb. This includes Khufu's amulet.

Cursed artifacts can be destroyed only if they are made very hot or very cold. Try throwing the amulet into a fire the next time you go camping.

You could also place the amulet in icy cold water. When it cracks, the curse will be lifted.

SURVIVING

Being cursed by a mummy is not ideal. But now you know how to fix it if it does happen.

In case of the rise of the mummies, keep this guide. It might even save your life!

30

GLOSSARY

afterlife the life a person has after their death

amulet a small object worn to protect the person wearing it

ancient very old

artifacts objects made long ago or from people in the past

booby traps hidden things made to stop or capture someone

curses things meant to cause trouble or bad luck to someone

legends stories that have been passed down from long ago but cannot be proven true

mummified prepared so a body lasts a long time

pharaohs kings or queens who ruled ancient Egypt

revenge payback for something that has been done

tomb a room where a dead body is laid to rest

torch a long stick with material at one end that burns brightly

Index

booby traps 8, 13, 17–18
curses 9–12, 20, 24–30
Egypt 4–6, 15–16
Giza 16
Khufu 16, 18–19, 28
pharaohs 4, 6–8, 11, 16
pyramids 4, 6–7, 13, 15–17, 24
Tutankhamun 11

Read More

Gieseke, Tyler. *Egyptian Mummies (Ancient Egypt).* Minneapolis: Abdo, 2022.

Spilsbury, Louise. *The Ancient Egyptians: Burials and Mummies (History's Horror Stories).* New York: Cavendish Square, 2020.

Learn More Online

1. Go to **www.factsurfer.com** or scan the QR code below.
2. Enter "**Rise of Mummies**" into the search box.
3. Click on the cover of this book to see a list of websites.